KALMUS ORGAN SERIES

1.50

WIDOR

SYMPHONY No. V
for the organ

Op. 42 No. 5

EDWIN F. KALMUS

PUBLISHER OF MUSIC

NEW YORK, N.Y.

974

WIDOR

SYMPHONY No. V
for the organ

Op. 42 No. 5

EDWIN F. KALMUS
PUBLISHER OF MUSIC
NEW YORK, N.Y.

SYMPHONIE V.
I.

Récit: Hautbois, Flutes 4, 16 — Positif: Montres et Gambes 8 — Grand-Orgue: Fonds 4, 8, 16.— Pédale: Basses 8, 16.

Allegro vivace. (β = 69)

Ch. M. Widor.

EDWIN F. KALMUS
PUBLISHER OF MUSIC
NEW YORK, N. Y.

a piacere a tempo

(Ped. Flûte 8 solo)

ritard.

Flûte 8

poco   a   poco   cresc.

16

II.

Grand orgue: Flute 8. Positif: Flutes 4. 8. Récit: Hautbois. Pédale: Basses 8. 16.

Allegro cantabile.

18

III.

G. Fonds 4. 8, 16. P. Fonds 4. 8. 16. R. Fonds 4. 8. P. Fonds 4, 8, 16, 32. Tous les claviers accouplés sur G.

Andantino quasi allegretto. (♩ = 88)

Ped. G P R

Ped. G P R

IV.

R: Gambe et voix céleste — G: Fonds de 8. 16. **Ped:** Flûte 4.

V.
Toccata.

Allegro. ($\downarrow$ = 100)

46

sempre staccato

diminuendo

181